Wakefield Press

a wild kind of tune

From her days as a botanist, to her years at
an agricultural school in Fiji, to her passion
for Australian rock art, Miriel Lenore has been
working away at questions of ecology and
place. Her poetry is also deeply grounded in her
experience as a feminist, mother, grandmother
and pioneer of a different sort.

This is Miriel Lenore's seventh book of poetry,
and the third volume in her Grandmothers trilogy,
following the success of *drums and bonnets* and
the Dog Rock. As in the earlier volumes, Miriel
continues to explore the heart-breaking questions
of the white settler story: where is home, how do
we live here?

Miriel Lenore lives in Adelaide.

T0363056

Much Madness is divinest Sense –
To a discerning Eye –
Much Sense – the starkest Madness –
'Tis the Majority
In this, as all, prevail –
Assent – and you are sane –
Demur – you're straightway dangerous
And handled with a chain –

Emily Dickinson 1863

a wild kind of tune

miriel lenore

**Wakefield
Press**

Wakefield Press
16 Rose Street
Mile End
South Australia 5031
www.wakefieldpress.com.au

First published 2015

Cover designed by Lahn Stafford Design
Text designed and typeset by Clinton Ellicott, Wakefield Press
Printed and bound by Griffin Press

National Library of Australia Cataloguing-in-Publication entry
Creator: Lenore, Miriel, author.
Title: A wild kind of tune / Miriel Lenore.
ISBN: 978 1 74305 370 6 (paperback).
Subjects: Lenore, Miriel – Family – Poetry.
                   Women – Australia – Poetry.
Dewey Number: A821.3

Publication of this book was assisted by
the Commonwealth Government through the
Australia Council, its arts funding and advisory body.

Contents

Preface

I first saw Caroline's name on an imposing gravestone in the Southern Tablelands of NSW:

Sacred to the Memory of William Southwell
Who died 25th June 1877
Also
Caroline beloved wife of the above
Who died 17th August 1908

Yet in 1908 Caroline had been Mrs. Samuel Edwards for thirty years.

Caroline was my great-grandmother. I was in high school when my mother whispered that Caroline had been in Hospitals for the Insane. Such was the shame of mental illness as the Twentieth Century began that, as a child, my mother was not told her grandmother was alive. She was an adult before she learnt that Caroline had been in mental hospitals for twenty-one years. What lies behind that brief revelation? What events shaped her earlier life? What complexities lurked behind the busy days of a pioneering household? How was she treated in those hospitals? When I saw the brevity of her entire medical record, I was horrified. This book began.

Caroline was the daughter of Tom and Sarah Brown, immigrants to Sydney in 1838. They soon settled in the Southern Tablelands of NSW where Caroline lived for most of her life.

a wild kind of tune is the third, after *drums & bonnets* and *the Dog Rock*, in my pioneer grandmothers series, unearthing the stories of women not famous, not wealthy, not beautiful, women who hold up half the sky.

The Southern Tablelands of NSW – Caroline's places

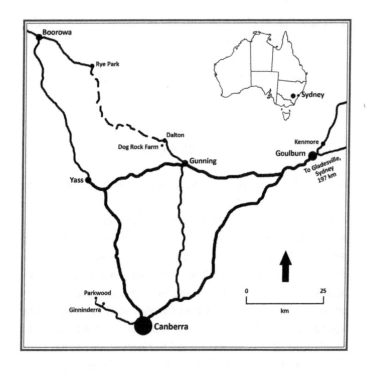

Chronology of Caroline Brown

23 July 1845, born at Stoney Range, Bringelly, NSW, the seventh child of Thomas and Sarah (Turk) Brown.

12th Oct 1845, she was baptised by Jonathan Innes at Bringelly.

1847, her family moved to Dog Rock Farm at Wesley Vale, later to be called Dalton, in NSW.

6th May 1863, Caroline married William Southwell at Dalton and lived at 'Parkwood', Ginninderra, where two children were born.

1867, they moved to Rye Park between Boorowa and Gunning and took up a settler block. Six more children were born.

25th June 1877, William died, aged 37.

23rd October 1878, Caroline married Samuel Edwards at Rye Park.

Four more children were born and one died (at 4 months) in 1881.

1885, just weeks after her twelfth child was born, Caroline had a manic attack and another in the following year.

24th October 1887, after a week-long attack, Caroline was admitted to *Gladesville Hospital for the Insane* suffering from *Mania Acute*.

14th August 1897, she was transferred to the 'model' *Kenmore Hospital* at Goulburn.

17th August 1908, Caroline died and was buried at Kenmore.

Travelling south 1837

Hard to leave the familiar for ever
harder to stay in Sussex with no money
uncertain work   their lives under threat
from riots and burning ricks

With their three young children
and a brother's family
Tom and Sarah sail for Sydney
expecting much from the land of promise

Hard those first years at the Cowpastures
harder after floods – so little food
and three more children to feed
They pray for pumpkins

Hard work labouring on Hassell's farms
harder as tenant farmers at Bringelly
where in 1845 Caroline is born

Before she can steadily walk
they will leave again the life they know
travelling south once more for land

Chapels

A family story has her baptised
in the famous Heber chapel
above the Nepean River
and the picturesque Vale of Denbigh

I want to believe that Tom and Sarah
brought Caroline to this sacred place
still part of Calcutta's Anglican Diocese
named for its Bishop who wrote
of his Asian see *Where every prospect
pleases and only man is vile*

But the family story is wrong

At the foot of the Stoney Range
in a chapel of *split slabs roofed with bark*
where Tom preached his *Boanerges
thunder, rattling his brimstone bag*
Caroline is received into the little band
of fervent Methodists

Bishop Heber's words are part of his once well-known hymn.

Boanerges, Aramaic for sons of thunder, was, according to the Bible,
used by Jesus for his disciples James and John. It became used to
describe a fiery orator.

En route

A very pregnant Sarah hauls herself
onto the already laden wagon
surrounds herself with the younger children
Caroline not yet two on her lap

They head south to the lands of promise

Overnight stops are a torture until Gunning
and a longer stay at nearby Stoney Hole
Tom rides off to find suitable land
Sarah gives birth to their eighth child

When Tom returns to announce success
the wagon is again piled high
Sarah nurses the baby   Caroline
is back with the bags of flour and sugar

Their journey ends at Oolong Creek

Dog Rock Farm

Lush grasses on alluvial flats
eucalypts and wattles on the slopes
occasional snows flooding down
Ngunawal people passing through

Oolong Creek bends to enclose a stage
for fastidious brolgas to dance
while dingoes howl on the rocky hill
which gave the farm its name

Now the sound of Tom's axe and gun
herald trees' and dingoes' fate The brolgas
vanish wheat and cows flourish on the flats
bushrangers and police passing through

Oolong Creek was named for the brolgas. Dog Rock Hill and Farm
were named by Tom Brown.

Under the honey tree
(*Eucalyptus mellidora*)

The eldest three children remember
Bringelly's paddocks though only Stephen
can recall the anxious voyage from Sussex

Caroline and the later children
simply know Dog Rock Farm as home
nestled in its sheltering cirque of granite

She joins the exuberant prayers and hymns
under the spreading honey tree
sees the farm expand and flourish
family too – with brothers sisters cousins

more Christians still for Wesley Vale
Later a town is born   and over all
from an immaculate blue sky
a Methodist God smiles

One month

No warnings on New Year's Day
1861 begins like any other
the farm prospering and settled
Children grow   the older ones marry

With her sister Sarah gone
Caroline at fifteen is now
the oldest daughter at home –
main helper with six young children

Her boisterous father is often away
preaching or carting goods
but garden house and church fill
pleasant days   there's enough to eat

Then suddenly   rampaging fevers
three sick children
pneumonic plague in the district
long frantic days and longer nights

Nine year old Mary dies first
then within weeks David at fourteen
and four-year-old Ebenezer
How many more?

Can she ever again expect to be safe?

Marriage

Few eligible men in County King
excluding Catholics and convicts of course
Luckily the Southwells at Ginninderra
a mere forty miles away provide
a quiverful of suitable offspring

Easy for handsome William at twenty-three –
carting goods back and forth to Sydney –
to visit these family friends just off the track
and see Caroline hard at work –
not yet eighteen   strong   personable
and Methodist – a perfect match

So they marry in the honey brick
church her father built
and leave for Ginninderra's Parkwood
where four young married couples
sleep in huts behind the homestead
companions in the kindly patriarch's realm

Ginninderra Falls

Yesterday we had a great picnic to a waterfall eighteen miles off.
I drove there, sketched, and rode back over fine grassy country . . .
we numbered in all seventeen riders.
– Constance Gordon Cumming, a Scottish visitor to Duntroon in 1875

The sketch is now a watercolour
in the National Library –
no falls but below organ-pipes of rock
a wide basin holds water soon to tumble
between boulders and stony banks towards
its junction with the Murrumbidgee
Scraggy eucalypts and sparse stands of native pine
are painted as a Scottish highland

Though the falls edge my ancestor's land
I doubt the party called on him:
more than miles separate
the wealthy graziers of Duntroon station
from the Methodist farmer at Parkwood

This land bears our family stories:
here is the hill where young Hannah
was lost then found by the Ngunawal
That hill was named for a favoured bullock
Thomas planted those willows and the sycamore
now on the Register of Significant Trees
Strange there are no stories of these

brisk disconcerting falls not guessed
from Parkwood's gentle slopes

I see the newly married Caroline
not yet eighteen   soon to be pregnant
running from the homestead's work and prayer
exulting in these untamed waters –
a quiet stream turned wild as it falls

I want the memory to stay with her
I want her to know that water
wears away stone
returns us all to the quiet depths of ocean

The epigraph is from *At Home in Fiji* (1881) by Constance Gordon
Cumming: The quotation is headed, DUNTROON, NEAR THE
MURRUMBIDGEE HILLS, N.S.WALES, Sept. 2 [1875]

A wild kind of tune

Hopping over the Clods is the family name for an unusual tune
to a well-known hymn by Charles Wesley.

1951
We are in my grandmother's Sydney house
for my mother's Jubilee celebration
a family tradition for 50th birthdays

Dinner is simple – no gourmets here
the jar of boiled lollies sits permanently
on the table

Family photos surround us on walls and dresser
with treasures like the silver vase
Mrs Hume of Everton gave Aunt Liza for sewing

The Bible follows the meal:
the Year of Jubilee is tonight's reading
before my grandmother prays

We move into the parlour for the customary
Jubilee gift – no longer fifty golden guineas
but fifty pounds (which still means ten weeks' work)

We stand around the piano –
my aunt plays so many tunes by ear
I request Hopping over the Clods

a wild kind of tune
ponderous but compelling
now become a family anthem:

Come, O thou all-victorious Lord,
Thy power to us make known;
Strike with the hammer of Thy Word
And break these hearts of stone.

When Caroline first sang it
in the early days of her marriage
I want to believe she was happy

must hope the hammer of the Word
brought her comfort before
the hammer of the Unsaid fell

Betsy Southwell, William's sister-in-law, brought an unusual tune with
her from Cawdor, near Camden, for a Wesley hymn. Ron Winch called it
'a strong, strange almost ponderous but still compelling tune that seems
to have no end; a wild kind of tune, almost as though it came from the
earth itself'. *Wattle Park 1882–1982*.

Uncle John Southwell, not otherwise known for flights of fancy, called
it Hopping over the Clods because of its bass.

The Hebrew Year of Jubilee, described in the Bible, (Leviticus25:vv 8–18
and later) began with the sound of 'trumpets of liberty' proclaiming the
liberation of all the inhabitants of the land; each person was to return to
the ancestral home, slaves to be set free, debts forgiven and land restored
to the previous owners. The Jubilee my family celebrated was a time for
family members to return home.

The celebration continued until the 1970s, siblings gathering
together at the family home. The person celebrating their 50th birthday
received fifty golden guineas, later pounds. I doubt they forgave debts or
returned land.

Driving to Rye Park

The Pajong walked this ancient road
towards Wirradjeri territory
settler wagons churned up mud
my car glides over gravel

Light-hearted I stop for lunch on a rise
near helter-skelter clumps of scribbly gums
where formal yakka dance in the breeze
holding erect their lightning rods

Behind me large rocks on the hillside
evoke the spirits of a past I can't enter
a history I was never taught –
my mood evaporates

Driving with William to her new home
Caroline passes the Wallabalooa camp
whose freedoms are diminishing faster
more completely than hers

William's sister

Mary Ann can reap an acre of wheat in a day
with her sickle
as good as a man the farmers say

Before fences   young Mary Ann
stays in the grasslands all day with the cows
bringing them home to milk

Her mother dies in childbirth   leaving her at 15
chatelaine of Parkwood   seven siblings to care for
including the baby who died at three months

At twenty she marries Alfred who'd grown up with her
goes with him to 'virgin land' on Pudman Creek
in Ngunawal territory   They call the place Rye Park

Rye for his English birthplace Park for her Parkwood home
Soon joined by William and Caroline as neighbours
I like to think they are comrades in hard times:

men building & felling & hoeing & sowing & reaping & carting
women cooking & feeding & washing & sewing & milking &
reaping & poultry & garden while breastfeeding   pregnant or both

Ten children in seventeen years   dead at thirty-seven
Mary Ann's headstone reads: *Thy will be done O Lord.*
Shall not the Judge of all the earth do right?

Memento mori

In a heavy frame above the fireplace
the huge print of William and Caroline
dominates the homestead dining room –
It's a wedding photo
my farmer cousin says
See he's too tired to stand
she's too sore to sit

There's no wedding here:
the Mitchell Library expert says my small print
was made from a carte de visite around 1872
the couple already married nine years
William Fearne was probably the photographer
he worked in Wagga and Yass

A very poor photo – the horizon's not level
chair carpet and cloth are props
probably that dress as well – it's too long for her
Yes a terrible photo he says of my treasure

This print is one of six on page 20 of a recent
family book: six grave Southwells in their thirties
with their father's heavy brows sit or stand beside
their solemn partners – the props re-used
two women wearing the same dress

Are they at Parkwood in 1873 for the patriarch's
sixtieth birthday when all seventy-one of the family

gather for food prayers and speeches
each grandchild receiving a shilling?

Caroline's face reveals little
she's placid or resigned like most of the wives:
life's no picnic but it could be worse

Married?

In the only photo of my great-grandparents
Caroline's pudgy fingers wear no rings –
strange for such worthy Methodists

Has she forgotten her wedding ring
in the race to get six children ready
for the long drive to a birthday party?

Has she already traded it to a passing hawker
like my mother who sold my father's
gold medals in the Depression?

Has it fallen into a pie while she cooked –
the fate of my own diamond
eaten I suppose by a dinner guest?

Was it lost in the cow yard?
Are her fingers too swollen to wear it?
Or is this a deliberate act of rebellion?

The road

In 1876 William gives land for a school:

*One acre and half of land Situated on the SW corner of
Mr A. Bembricks 35 acres. running East by West 4 chains
and running 3 chains 3/4 North by South. with a reserved
road for Public purposes situated on the South side.*

The Education Council asks for a plan. He sends one with the
width of the exempted road shown as 1 rod, then he adds a tiny
'o' above, making it 1 rood, measure of area not width.

The council asks the width of the road.
Again William sent the answer:

1 rood ... it his more convenient for water purposes ...

Again and again the letters, William's getting terser each time
Again the council:

Please state the width of the road.

William has had enough:

Rye Park 30th May 1876
Sir
*i cannot give a more correct statement. than i have already
sent to you.*
*2nd I stated in my last letter that the road i wished for 1 rood
wide was my Private land. and private ideas also. had i have
known the giving of 1 acre and 1/2 of my land to the Council
of Education for School purposes would have been attended
with such great trouble to the Council of Education and
myself, i should have much rather have kept it.*
*When the first description of the land was sent it fully
described the road the rest appears to me a complete*

humbug on one side or the other i cannot say which
only that hit is very discouraging for a man to be
liberal in such cases.
I beg to remain yours etc
William Southwell
Education Council to solicitors:
Mr Southwell evidently intends that the width of the
road should be 1 rod not one rood.

Within a year, William is dead at 37.
I am told it was probably peritonitis, not choler.

Intestate

How can William
father of eight
die without a will?
Even a speedy end
usually allows
for a brief note

So much trouble
so easily avoided –
Is mortality
at thirty-seven
too terrible
to contemplate?

He can't foresee
the long years' wait
before the family
can inherit his land

Rye Park cemetery

The dead long to be of use:
read their tombstones
Stop traveller and cast an eye
For as you are so once was I . . .

Be therefore ready . . .

Lost babies are everywhere
Safe in the arms of Jesus –
children only of their fathers it seems
except for the *child of Miss Palmer*

Amongst the Ngunawal families –
the Russells the Lewises the Lanes –
lie *Aborigine* and *Mary Aborigine*
and in the farthest corner *Old Jack* –
recent historians have done their best
the plaques are quite new

His sons claim most for William:
Mark the Perfect Man . . .
When their father died their ages
ranged from eleven to two

Fate

Caroline needs help after William's death –
impossible to manage a farm
with eight children in her care
Her brother comes but can't stay:
he has their mother's land to work

At Crago's Flour Mills in Yass
two men read notices on the wall:
two widows require workers for their farms
They toss – and Sam Edwards goes to Caroline

Sam at twenty-eight   hare-lipped red-haired
and strong   is grateful he can bring
his little boy whose mother said *I carried him
nine months; it's your turn now*   and left

Within a year there is a wedding

The second husband

Sam fancies her daughter Liza
the first day he comes to help
the new widow on her farm

Uncouth and inarticulate
he yearns to marry the young girl
Within the year asks the mother
for her hand   But the widow herself
accepts him – or so her grandson
    says

Is Sam too clumsy to explain
or like Humbert Humbert
does he take his only chance?
He comes up from the paddocks
for his lunchtime wedding
goes straight back to the crops

The new bride and groom share
the tiny hut with the beloved Liza
her sister Hannah six brothers
aged two to twelve and Sam's young son

Over the next seven years
the widow has four children with Sam
while he moons over her daughter
fights with her teenage sons

Humbert Humbert is the protagonist of Vladimir Nabokov's 1955
novel *Lolita*, which explored an older man's obsession with a young
girl and his marriage to her mother as a way of being near her.

Mrs Southwell's fence

Rye Park Janu 24th 79
To the Council of Education
Sir

in reference to the present old fencing which
stands upon that acre and half which the Late Mr
William Southwell Gave to the Council for School
purposes. Mrs Southwell says Mr William Southwell
her Late husband never intended to Give the fence
that was on the ground but kindly let it remain until
the Council of Education put a better one. under this
circumstance is the fencing the Council property or
Mrs Southwell would the council be kind enough to
deside this matter and let me know there is about 50
pannel of fencing

I have the honour to be
Sir
Your most obedient servant
Charles Plumb
Secretary

Six months later, the answer comes:
The school site was conveyed unconditionally,
so the fencing belongs to the Council.

In 1879 Caroline is Mrs Edwards not Southwell
Does the school council hope the donor's widow
may be heard more favourably?

Is Sam consulted
or is this an early example
of his outsider position in the village?
An erasure completed when Caroline's name
is on William Southwell's gravestone

Alfred Campbell Edwards

Red veins in the leaves above the tiny grave
where the four month old baby lies
Caroline's second child with Sam

A rounded marble headstone
bears no name no parents' names
two words only: OUR BABY

If he had lived perhaps their world
of anger lust and grief might have dissolved
in his engaging smile

Madness

Caroline has three short bursts
of wild frenzy – three weeks
within three years
the first after her twelfth child's birth

The final explosive week in 1887
sends her to Gladesville Hospital
for committal with no parole
confinement until death

The Gladesville Records

How to enter my great-grandmother's world?
Madness is too big for me

1
Gladesville Hospital for the Insane:
Records of Caroline Edwards
No of Register 1696   **Case Book L**   **Folio No 2**

I the undersigned hereby request you to receive

Caroline Edwards   *an insane person into the Hospital
for the Insane of which you are the Superintendent*

Samuel Edwards   *Name of person signing the request*

Farmer   *Occupation (if any) of that person*

Rye Park   *Place of his Abode*

Husband   *Degree of relationship (if any) or other
circumstances of connection*

*Dated this 24th day of October one thousand eight hundred
and Eighty Seven*

Signature of person making request   *Samuel Edwards*

Witness to signature   *A D Fanne Canon C E
R Williams JP*

To F N Manning Esq
Superintendent of the Hospital for the Insane
at Gladesville

These records are the complete transcription of the Hospital Records of Caroline's
time at Gladesville and Kenmore.

2

Statement respecting the said   *Caroline Edwards*

Name in full   Caroline Edwards

Age   Forty two years

Married, single, or widowed?   Married

Number of children?   Twelve

Age of youngest child?   Four years

Previous occupation   Domestic

Native place?   Camden NSW

Late residence   Rye Park

Religious persuasion?   Wesleyan

Supposed course of insanity?   Not known

How long has the attack lasted   One week

Has she been insane before?   Yes

State the number of attacks   Twice

Age (if known) at first attack   Thirty nine years

Has she any insane relatives   No

Has she ever been an inmate
of any institution for the insane?   No

Is she subject to fits?   No

Is she suicidal?   No

Is she dangerous to others?   No

Special circumstances (if any) preventing the
patient being examined before admission
separately by two medical practitioners

(Signed)   Samuel Edwards

(Address)   Rye Park Burrowa

3

Committed to prison after her third short attack
Did she go to Sydney by train?
Was she bound?
Were the police her gaolers?
Were they kind?
Did family travel with her?
Not Sam –
all writing on the form including
his signature and the witnesses'
is in the same hand

4

Admitted October 31st 1887

1887 Nov 7

Before admission: Medical Certificates state
she was violent, destructive, incoherent & dirty
in her habits, refuses food and was generally
unable to take care of herself
In the R. H (6 days). She was restless
troublesome and dirty.

On and during admission:
She is an ill-nourished middle aged woman
whose mental condition is one of Acute Mania.
She has grey eyes, brownish hair, a straight nose,
several teeth absent and a sallow complexion.

All her systems are apparently normal.
She is absolutely incoherent, violent,
destructive and dirty in her habits
and very troublesome generally.

She takes her food fairly well
but rests indifferently at night

The RH may mean The Royal Hospital for Women.

5

Before admission *refuses food*
but in hospital *She takes her food fairly well*
Is the refusal a sign of rebellion
or after a lifetime of preparing meals
is she saying that's enough with food?
If others prepare it that's different

generally unable to take care of herself
What is the family to do –
Sam at work on the farm
Liza busy in house and farm?
Perhaps committal is all they can manage

Acute Mania
Is this how she met stress?
With a gene from her father –
Tom the fool for God
Tom the man who killed a man
Tom the always repenting sinner?
Was it post-partum psychosis?
A hormone or chemical in the brain?
Was it grief?   So many deaths
A terrible despair?
Was it escape?

She is an ill-nourished middle-aged woman
Was it malnutrition?
Did her body finally give way

after twelve children in eighteen years
pregnant and breastfeeding together?

several teeth absent
'every child a tooth' our mothers said
as their babies drained their calcium

absolutely incoherent, violent, destructive
I like to think that painful energy
banked for so long
surged out at last as rage
to give her spirit some relief

6

1887	*Nov 14*	*no change*
	Nov 21	*do*
	Nov 28	*no change*
	Dec 5	*do*
	Dec 31	*no change*
1888	*Jan 31*	*do*
	Feb 29	*do*
	Mar 31	*do*
	Jun 30	*do*
	Aug 31	*do*
	Nov 30	*do*
1889	*Feb 28*	*do*
	May 31	*do*

The '*do*' of various dates is presumably 'ditto'.

7

no change

No change in eighteen months –
could nothing be said?
health? weight? behaviour? speech?
No treatment at all?

8

1889   August 31   Has improved in so far that she is quiet

         Nov 30   do

9

Has improved in so far that she is quiet
Improved?

After the raging years she took the only way
withdrew into herself and shut the door

Why couldn't she be like her brother Benjamin
who lasted in such captivity just one week?

Caroline's younger brother Benjamin was admitted to Callan Park,
a Mental Institution in Sydney while Caroline was in Gladesville.
He died within a week after being very ill and passing blood.

10

1890	Feb 28	no change		
	Mar 31	do	June 30	do
	Sept 30	do	Dec 31	do
1891	Mar 31	do	June 30	do
	Sept 30	do	Dec 31	do
1892	"	"	"	"
1893	"	"	"	"
1894	"	"	"	"
1895	Mar 31	do		
	June 30	She continues in a state of chronic mania		
1896	Mar 31	do	June 30	do
	Sept 30	do	Dec 31	do
1897	Mar 31	She shows no mental improvement		

11
chronic mania   no mental improvement
Two short sentences in seven years
No illness in that time? No attempts at speech?

I hope her spirit went back to Dog Rock
and the loving years of childhood
to Ginninderra's wild falls
the companionable years of early marriage
even to the first years of shared work
at Rye Park with William
no perhaps not there:
too close to the troubled years of Sam's reign

Liza

With Caroline safely in Gladesville
Sam attained his dream
for Liza must stay with the children

She hated the fighting
helped her brothers leave the farm
escape from Sam's severity

Yet when they had gone
and her home sold
she stayed with Sam

What did she feel for this man
who drove away two suitors
with shotgun and fiery threats
who loved her for over fifty years?

She called him Dearie

The brothers

Because William left no will
and Caroline couldn't act
the inheritance was frozen
until they were twenty-one
By then all had left the farm
soured by their fights with Sam

Jabez hacked his farm out of bush
the other side of town
John went to a block across the creek
David was far away offering
salvation to miners
Joe and William worked in shops
And Amos cut chaff

The girls of course could not leave –
Liza and Hannah stayed in their parents' house
with Sam and the three youngest children

When the administrators finished
Joe inherited the home block
hurried to sell it
failed to tell his sisters

The new owner had to report that Liza
the children – and Sam – were homeless
They took a small cottage in the village
went to the same church on Sunday
sang the same hymns as the brothers
who never spoke to them

The organ

Not enough you'd think to split a church
but religion brings out the wildest feelings
It seemed as if God had personally decreed

that hymns should be led and sung line by line –
the devil was in the asthmatic sounds
from the newly installed pedal organ

Some left the church when the organ came –
the son of an early pioneer and Sam too
though Liza was the first organist

They asked the new Salvation Army to come –
strange when trumpets and drums outdid the organ
but accepted by God I suppose like King David's dancing

The reference to King David dancing in front of the ark of God is in the
Bible (2 Samuel 6:vv 5,14).

The clearing sale

The whole district
is at Cookes' clearing sale
Sam spies the brothers in the crowd
shouts at his loudest –
his usually indistinct speech
sharp enough for all to hear
Why don't you pay for your mother?

My cousin tells the story with a laugh
it seems the brothers never offered
to help with the costs
There's no lingering embarrassment

The Kenmore Records

Gladesville Hospital for the insane: Caroline Edwards

1897 June 14 She was this day transferred to Kenmore

1
Kenmore Hospital for the Insane –
the new enlightened place on a rise
above the Wollondilly River
at Goulburn City of Lilacs
where fresh air and exercise
could cure the troubled souls

Too late for Caroline who saw no lilacs
who came in winter cold
to harsh winds and occasional snow
unheated wards and freezing corridors

Did they give her warm clothes?
I couldn't bear for her to be mad and cold

Much nearer now to her family
did they visit?
Not Sam though he paid her costs of
seventeen shillings and four pence monthly

Perhaps her sons?
David the Salvationist came
on his annual leave from Victoria –
the one who called his daughter Caroline

2

Kenmore Hospital for the Insane:
Records of Caroline Edwards (310)

1897 June 21   She is a fairly well nourished middle aged
woman in fairly robust health, mentally in a condition of
advanced dementia.

She is silent,
takes no interest in her surroundings
and apparently has no idea of her whereabouts,
is often faulty in her habits, unable to do any useful work,
has no power of initiative and simply vegetates from
day to day.

She rests quietly at night.

3

She rests quietly at night
Blissful sleep   no nightmares
no dreams that disturb
no guilty conscience
She has retreated from the stress
of love and hate

4

1897	June 28	no change				
1897	July 5th	no change	12th	do		
	19	do	26th	do	31	do
	Aug 31	do	Sept	do	Oct 30	do
1898	Jan 31	do	April 30	the same		
	June 20th	the same				
	Sept 30th	The same. Habits faulty, puts rubbish in her ears etc.				

5

puts rubbish in her ears
After such silence did the voices return?
Even here they follow   Is there no pity?

What does she find to fill her ears
in those empty wards?
A piece of cloth? Bits of string?
Paper scraps? Dirt and pebbles from the yard?

What noise does she wish not to hear?
Do the shouts and bad words
of the farm come back?
The softness of Sam's words to Liza
the boys' defiant tones?

6

1898	Dec 31st	The same		
1899	Mar 31st	The same	June 27th	The same
	Sept 22nd	The same	Dec 15th	same
1900	Mar 31st	same	June 4th	same
	4.9.00	same	4.12.00	very demented
1901	Mar 4th	Demented, dirty in her habits silent.		
	June 1st	Faulty in habits demented, and idle.		
	Sept 1st	Mentally unchanged		
	Dec 1st	Idle, untidy in dress		

7

demented and idle
She had worked hard all her life –
now she could be idle so she would
First time she'd ever been served
had food brought to her
I hope in some corner of her mind
she knew and was happy

1902	Mar 1st	remains the same		
	June 1st	no change		
	Sept 1st	The same	Dec 1st	same

1903	Mar 1st	Faulty in habits		
	June 1st	do		
	Sept 1st	do	Dec 1st	No change

| 1904 | 1.3.04 | No change | 1.6.04 | remains the same |
| | 1.9.04 | No change | 1.12.04 | no change |

| 1905 | Mar 1 | Remains the same | June 1 | No change |
| | Sept 1 | No change | | |

1905   Dec 1   Her memory for time and place is bad.
Questions need repeating several times before
an answer can be got
and that is generally "I don't know".
Her volitional power is paralysed
and her reactions slow or absent.
Her social ethical and aesthetic feelings
are destroyed.
She understands what is said to her.
She is slow in her movements.
She is idle and dirty and says
she is wrong in the head.

9

She understands what is said to her
says she is wrong in the head
So she is still present capable of response

In her nine years at Kenmore
seven people wrote her reports
Only the scribe of 1905
took her seriously gave us a portrait

After asylum for eighteen years
she knew she was *wrong in the head* –
a sentence requiring some capacity
What if others in 1887 had drawn her out
talked with her   uncovered her pain?
Did three separate weeks of rage
deserve twenty-one years of prison?

She understands what is said to her.
So her silence was a deliberate rebellion
a retreat to the music of garden and orchard
Oolong Creek   the surrounding hills
the falls at Ginninderra

10

1906	Mar 1	No change	June 1	No change
	Sept 1	No change	Dec 1	No change
1907	Mar 1	No change	June 1	No change
	Sept 1	No change	Dec 1	No change
1908	March 1	No change	June 1	No change

11

One other person showed interest
in the ailing patient: a note and a small graph
record her weight loss

Female	2 Sept 1906	weight 8.7	Nov 1906	7.11
	Jan 1907	7.10	Apr 1907	7.10
	Aug 1907	7.4	June 1908	6.12½

Inheritance

she has only to show her hands to heaven and she'll
be welcomed in   — Liza's sister, Hannah

Liza's land beside the school
            is Superb Parrot country
where sheep graze among old red gums
            along the Pudman Creek

Across the Rugby Road Liza grew
            fodder for her cows –
nieces remember her and Sam
      with reaping hooks at harvest time
companionable under a golden sun

When Caroline was sent to Gladesville
            Liza at twenty-two
had care of a sick sister   a slow sister
five young brothers   and Sam

After the brothers left she still cared for Sam
            two sisters and the little half-brother
she treated as a son:
I have the opal he later mined and gave her

In their cottage in the village she helped
                  keep the family
with sales of eggs and butter returning at last light
with the cows
Sam's grandchildren remember her work-worn hands
gently applying mustard plasters that burnt the skin
wet cloths to soothe their fevered heads

David's share

I was impressed when told my grandfather David
gave six acres in the main street
for Rye Park showground and sports reserve –
a generous act from a Salvation Army officer
who kept his household of twelve on one pound a week –
not surprised a condition was imposed
'no Sunday sport': his grandfather at Parkwood
once rebuked a visiting preacher
for walking in the garden on the Sabbath

Now I learn the land was sold
for £19.10 with no conditions
the absent Salvationist taking the blame
for the Council's unpopular ban

Two myths scotched at the same time
I eat my lunch under a large gum
in the Reserve my grandfather sold
could play Sunday tennis if I chose

The red chair

Her brothers couldn't ignore Liza's Jubilee birthday
After all they owed her for long years of caring
(their mother always nursing a new child)
and she in charge after Caroline was sent away
Anyway it *was* a family tradition

But they couldn't celebrate her
wouldn't forgive her either
still living with Sam caring for Sam
perhaps even loving Sam
and certainly she loved his children
She *deserved* the distance they kept

In the end the brothers thought of a way –
they bought a red-plush armchair
left it without a word
on the veranda of her cottage

Silently it was taken inside
Later Sam's grand-children
remember this chair as special
recall Sam resting on it
Liza never

The Final Records
Kenmore Hospital for the Insane

1

1908   August 17 She died this day

2

NSW Death Certificate:

Caroline Edwards aged 63

Cause of death (a) *cardiac disease*   (b) *senility*

Buried *18th August 1908*

Kenmore Hospital Cemetery Goulburn

Name and Religion of Minister: *Michael Bembrick   Methodist*

3

Buried the day after her death
she finally escaped her unfair life
No family followed her to the grave
no time even if they wanted to
Yet by chance a nephew was there:
as local minister he blessed her
in her pauper's grave

4

Raging Caroline quiet Caroline
dead Caroline
is not forgotten
Her sons added her name
to their father's large monument
and my mother and my daughter
carry that name

Two Carolines

Seven years apart two Carolines
were born in the Southern Tablelands
Both married at eighteen   lived in the same district
and had twenty-two children between them
They died of heart complaints within a month
their memorials are in the cemetery
behind Rye Park Methodist church

'Queen' Caroline an elder of the Ngunuwal
was the matriarch of the place
related to the Hume family of Everton
daughter of Bridget Collins of the Pajong
and a 19 year-old squatter John Chisholm

A survivor in both worlds she owned land
(portion 29 in the parish of Upton)
was buried between two daughters
A huge procession followed her to the grave:
four decorated black horses pulling a grand hearse
her coffin made by settler friends who assisted at the burial
Some mourners wailed and chanted   others stiffly silent
as the cortege turned at the top of the village
to pass through Methodist grounds to the cemetery

The priest would not enter such heretical territory
went down a side lane   jumped the fence
and sprinkled holy water on the ground
ready to receive his parishioner

The other Caroline
daughter of Sarah Turk and Thomas Brown
wife of William Southwell and Sam Edwards

is not in the grave bearing her name
Her bones are still at Kenmore
the sad woman who couldn't control her rages
who failed to survive her difficult world
as wife mother farmer widow

Matriarch to no one in spite of twelve children
no family came for her funeral
no fine coffin   no long procession
One link only with home –
the minister her nephew

The unhappy sons engraved
the words AT REST below her name
on their father's substantial monument

From the Family Bible

Eliza Southwell Died at Rye Park April 21 aged 70 1935
I know first when she was 14 years and from that time
she was a faithful Christian loyal woman and for only
1 year 6 months was the longest time she was away from me

Through times of sickness and times fighting those who
have been friends was loyal beyond my powers to express
her love and faithfulness God will bless
to day her spirit is in Paridise where I know I meet her soon
Lord I beseech Thee for Jesus Name
Samuel Edwards

A teacher found him hanging
from the veranda cut him down to live
four long years without his love –

On her grave a white plaster dove
encased in an everlasting glass dome
and on her headstone the words:
A FAITHFUL AND LOVING FRIEND OF 58 YEARS

in the new and empty cemetery
he arranged for a grave behind hers
so their headstones could touch

Divisions

There were always fights and factions
in this small place of strong opinions
Caroline's son Stephen was left out
of family parties since he went to dances
and married an Anglican
Anyway he was Sam's son
Sam cut his granddaughter from his will
for marrying a Catholic
his own exclusion teaching him nothing
Even after he died a world war starting
and religious sentiment less vehement
divisions remained

Now William's land is in Catholic hands
both sides of Caroline's family pray together
unite to welcome distant relatives

Church

Unusual
especially with Methodist folk
for Ngunawal and settlers
to attend the same church

But the neighbouring farmers
along the Creek
sang Sunday hymns together
in the local school

Caroline Southwell's grandson led
the service   prayed God to forgive
them their sins – like us aware of
some and unaware of others

Kids peeked between their fingers
longing to lark about outside
playing marbles skippy hopscotch
or jacks

Both Carolines were dead
when their great-grandchildren
played together   not yet mindful
of distances other than geographical

Tempus etc

Every relic of Caroline's hut has gone
but her fruit trees still flaunt white blossom
at the surrounding pasture

Liza's cottage where she lived with Sam
is straggling boards and sheets of iron
the dairy more substantial than the house

Rusted roof broken windows and slanting posts
mark the bigger house that Sam's son
Stephen built with Liza's gift

The church is still neat and kempt
its clear lancet windows outlined in white
gnomish and wide-awake

Its message is harder to read:
modest Mt Snowdon rises behind the creek
Mt Misery is further to the north

Kenmore Hospital Cemetery

I want to see my great-grandmother's grave
The man in the office is embarrassed:
we are going to fix it
you'll need someone to show you
I wait till the farm manager can take me
across several paddocks to a small
unkempt area hidden by pines

There are hollows among ordered rows
of unnamed wooden pegs
is Caroline here?
Oh no he says *these are Japanese soldiers*
this was a military hospital in the war

Not Cowra?   There the Japanese war dead
lie in precision rows
beside symbolic cryptomeria
planted by the Emperor's sons
an altar to ease the warrior's passage
It's different he says *these soldiers were mad*

Somewhere beyond the pines
under tall thistles and weeds
Caroline lies with the unquiet dead
casualty of a different war

Victoria Cross

Alone in his house now surrounded by
vacant home sites and crumbled buildings
his land has shrunk to a village block
holding bees chooks and one lamb

Caroline's grandson can see across
the paddocks to the twelve remaining
fruit trees (one for each of her children)
which mark the place of her slab hut

Those days were just too hard
He doesn't want to dig up the past
or talk of Caroline's life except to say
Sometimes the wrong people get the VC

The ring

I inherited from my mother a ruby ring
she said belonged to Caroline
My aunt thinks they were too poor for rings
could it be a blood-red garnet?

I want it to be Caroline's
I'm sure it's hers –
her one legacy to her daughter
left when she was certified

Now no one knows
I'll keep my mother's story
my daughter Caroline has the ring
symbol of fire and blood   love and life

Acknowledgements

So many people have helped me search for my great-grandmother Caroline. My thanks to members of her family, especially my relatives Winnie Veness, Sylvia Pearsall, Pam and Jim Grace, Garry and Lillian Southwell, Roland, Albert and Alf Southwell and the late Avis Mansell, who provided stories, information and hospitality. I enjoyed letters from the late Ron Edwards. However the portrait of Caroline is my own.

I am grateful for the support and advice of Louise Crisp, Diane Fahey, Margaret Merrilees, Jill Golden, Annette Marner and Kaz Eaton. Thanks also to Sandra Taylor who drew the map of Caroline's part of NSW. My family and friends are unfailingly encouraging and Ruth Raintree has my special thanks for all her support in so many ways to this project and to me.

Thanks again to Michael Bollen and all at Wakefield Press for our sixth book together, especially to Clinton Ellicott who has designed and typeset most of them, and Katherine Lahn who has designed the covers for the three Grandmother books.

Wakefield Press is an independent publishing and
distribution company based in Adelaide, South Australia.
We love good stories and publish beautiful books.
To see our full range of books, please visit our website at
www.wakefieldpress.com.au
where all titles are available for purchase.

Find us!

Twitter: www.twitter.com/wakefieldpress
Facebook: www.facebook.com/wakefield.press
Instagram: instagram.com/wakefieldpress